LET'S GET CRACKING!

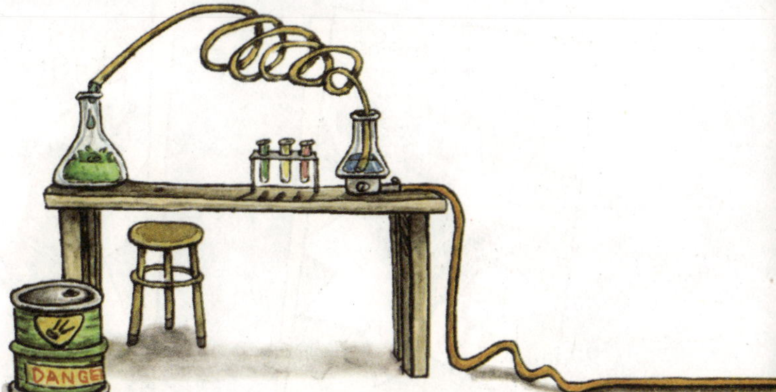

Read more Kung Pow Chicken books!

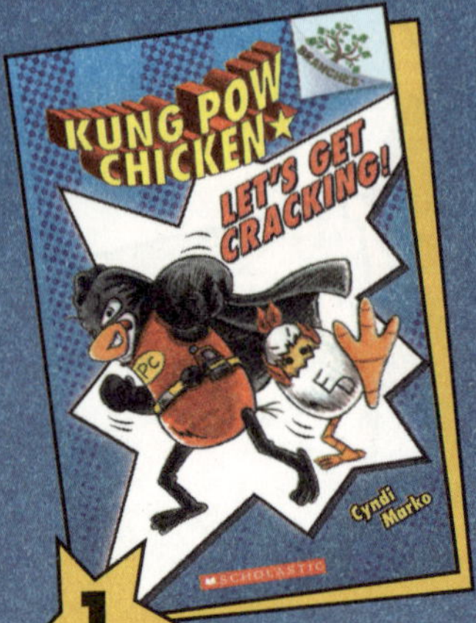
KUNG POW CHICKEN
LET'S GET CRACKING!
Cyndi Marko
SCHOLASTIC

1

KUNG POW CHICKEN
BOK! BOK! BOOM!
Cyndi Marko
SCHOLASTIC

2

KUNG POW CHICKEN
THE BIRDY SNATCHERS
Cyndi Marko
SCHOLASTIC

3

KUNG POW CHICKEN
HEROES ON THE SIDE
Cyndi Marko
SCHOLASTIC

4

KUNG POW CHICKEN★

LET'S GET CRACKING!

Cyndi Marko

BRANCHES™
SCHOLASTIC INC.

For Liam,
who is always willing to laugh at my bad egg jokes and, more often than not, offer one of his own

Library of Congress Cataloging-in-Publication Data

Marko, Cyndi, author, illustrator.
Let's get cracking! / by Cyndi Marko.
pages cm. — (Kung Pow Chicken ; 1)
Summary: Gordon Blue and his brother Benny, unlikely superheroes, must save Fowladelphia from Granny Goosebumps, who has filled the city with cookies that cause innocent chickens' feathers to fall off.
ISBN 9789351034308
Superheroes—Juvenile fiction. 2. Chickens—Juvenile fiction. 3. Cookies—Juvenile fiction. [1. Superheroes—Fiction. 2. Chickens—Fiction. 3. Cookies—Fiction. 4. Humorous stories.] I. Title. II. Title: Let us get cracking.
PZ7.M33968Let 2014
813.6—dc23
2013018130

12 11 10 9 8 7 6 5 4 3 2 1 14 15 16 17 18 19/0

First Printing January 2014,
Reprint October 2014, January 2015
Reprinted by Scholastic India Pvt. Ltd.
Printed at: Saurabh Printers Pvt. Ltd.

TABLE OF CONTENTS

superhero
poster
ROCKET
ROOSTER
supersonic
rocket
bunny
slippers
drum

Enter The Chicken 1

Gordon Blue seemed like an ordinary chicken.

Gordon was in second grade at an ordinary school.

He lived in an ordinary house in the ordinary city of Fowladelphia. But he had a <u>super</u> secret.

Only Uncle Quack and Gordon's younger brother, Benedict, knew Gordon's secret.

Uncle Quack was a scientist. He worked in a lab.

One day when Gordon and Benny were younger, they had visited Uncle Quack at work.

Gordon and Benny started playing Follow the Leader. Gordon was in the lead and Benny followed every move Gordon made. Then . . .

. . . Gordon tripped and fell into a huge vat of bubbling toxic sludge! Benny followed Gordon's lead.

Uncle Quack quickly rescued his nephews.

Maybe we won't tell your mom about this. . . .
buy $ pluto-nium
library books due!

But later Gordon started to feel strange. And as time passed he felt even stranger.

He tingled when danger was near.

He flapped his wings like the wind.

And he crowed louder than other chickens. His bok was worse than his bite.

Gordon was no longer just an ordinary chicken. The toxic sludge had given him superpowers.

Hey, I got powers, too!
My shell is harder than
cafeteria cookies!

So Gordon made a super suit.

Hey, where's mine?

And Gordon came up with a super name:

KUNG POW CHICKEN!
Sidekicks always get left out! I'm Egg Drop, and I'm super, too!
KP
ED

Gordon promised to use his powers to right wrongs, to fight bad guys, and to keep his room <u>super</u> clean.

Superhero promises
1. be super nice.
2. be super good.
3. be super tidy.
Egg Drop
Kung Pow Chicken

But Gordon hadn't met any bad guys yet. So he still had to do ordinary chicken things, like go to school.

Sunny-Side Up! 2

Today was a bright fall day and Gordon was <u>super</u> excited about the school field trip to the Fowl Fall Festival.

Gordon's mother straightened his school tie and handed him his lunch box.

Gordon carried his lunch box everywhere. But he never let anyone see what was inside.

It's a bit nippy out today, Gordie. You'd better wear your hat.
But that hat messes up my comb!

Mrs. Blue gave Gordon her very best mom stare. Gordon put on the hat.

Before her kids could escape, Mrs. Blue looped a scarf around Benny. Then she covered both Gordon and Benny in kisses.

Stay together on your field trip today, boys!
Mom! Let go!

Gordon and Benny walked to school.

Ham and eggs! I hope Mom never finds out we're superheroes.
Me too! She'd never let us leave the house again!

When Gordon and Benny got to school, they joined their classmates out front. Everyone was excited to go to the Fowl Fall Festival.

Finally, the school bus arrived.

When they got to the festival, Gordon's teacher, Mr. Giblets, gave a long talk about rules.

Balloons
CANDY CORN
. . . No pecking or shoving
bok, bok, bok . . .
stay with your buddy
bok, bok, bok . . . best behavior
bok, bok, bok . . .

Gordon and Benny were ready to burst. Gordon wanted to see the magician. Benny wanted to eat candy corn. And they both wanted to have a cookie.

Then Gordon's beak started to twitch. And his tail feathers began to wiggle.

TINGLE!

Gordon could tell something was wrong, <u>very</u> wrong.

My birdy senses are tingling. . . . Someone must be up to no good!

3 A Foul Festival

How do we find anything in this crowd?
Just keep looking. Bad guys can't hide for long!

Gordon and Benny pushed through the large flock of chickens. They were on the lookout for bad guys.

Suddenly, clucks and feathers filled the air. Gordon stared open-beaked. Everywhere he looked, feathers were blasting off chickens with a loud POOF!

POOF!
I've got chickenbumps!
BOK!
POOF!
Don't you mean goosebumps? Chickenbumps isn't a word!
But I'm a chicken and I have bumps!
BOK!
POOF!

BOK!
POOF!
BOK!
POOF!
Gordon, this is our chance to be heroes!
I've got my lunch box! Let's find a place to hide!

Quick!
In here!

They dashed inside. Gordon flung open his lunch box. . . .

KPC

Ack! Leotard wedgie!

A few seconds later, Kung Pow Chicken and his sidekick, Egg Drop, burst into action!

LET'S GET CRACKING!
HI-YAH!
KP
ED

Kung Pow Chicken and Egg Drop searched for clues and talked to naked chickens.

What is that you're eating, sir?
BOK!
The worst cookie ever!
Excuse me, did you just eat something?
BOK!
BOK!
KPC
Yes! A yucky cookie!

Ham and eggs! Look! Weird glowy cookies!

The naked chickens all must have eaten those cookies!
Now let's find the bad guys!

ITCH
Granny Goosebumps's Warm Woolies
ITCH

The heroes looked high and low for any sign of the bad guys. Then they spotted a busy booth selling hand-knit sweaters. Chilly naked chickens were scrambling to buy the sweaters.

My birdy senses are doing the Funky Chicken! That granny must be up to no good!
KP

Kung Pow Chicken sneaked in for a closer look.

But he was spotted!

ZOING!
Eat yarn, dearie!
bumps's woolies

I'm trapped!
Egg Drop . . . STOP, DROP, AND THUNDER ROLL!

Egg Drop stopped. He dropped. And he rolled like thunder. . . .

BLAMMO!
Granny

Kung Pow Chicken burst free of the tangled trap. He flashed his Drumsticks of Doom!

I'm Kung Pow Chicken!
You are doomed to go to jail!
KAPOW!

I'm Granny Goosebumps! My Naughty Knitting Needles will have you in stitches!

Granny Goosebumps used her Naughty Knitting Needles to fling yarn at Kung Pow Chicken. He plucked the spinning yarn out of the air with his drumsticks. Then he became locked in a battle of knits with the grumpy granny.

PFFT!
KNIT!

Granny Goosebumps, your goose is cooked!
PURL!
KPC
Think again, dearie!
KPC
OVER!
CHOP!
UNDER!
ZING!

Granny Goosebumps threw Kung Pow Chicken to the ground.

Suddenly, some other grannies came crashing through the crowd. They scooped up Granny Goosebumps and sped away!

Mwa-ha-ha!
COOKIES
COOKIES
COOKIES
COOKIE

So Granny Goosebumps isn't just selling sweaters! She's also selling those crummy cookies! But why? And why are those other grannies helping her?
Let's follow them, Kung Pow! . . . Hey, what's wrong?
I don't feel very super. I want to go home.

Gordon Hides Out

4

On the bus ride home, Gordon didn't want to talk. Outside, the city itched for a hero.

As soon as Gordon got home, he went straight to his room.

He put on his favorite bunny slippers.

He snuggled under his favorite blanket.

And he read his favorite comic book.

Benny knocked on Gordon's door.

Sigh.
Gordon, you have to get up!
GORDON'S ROOM
go away
No way! I can't do it. I tried. I'm just not a hero.

Ham and eggs, Gordon! You're a superhero! If you won't fight bad guys, who will?

Gordon knew Benny was right. He needed to be brave because the city needed his help. And no crummy cookie or grumpy granny was going to stop him. He grabbed his lunch box.

I am Kung Pow Chicken . . . and Granny Goosebumps had better mind her manners.

Gordon and Benny found their mother in the kitchen.

Mom? Can we go for a bike ride?
Yes, but you'd better be back in time for dinner.
YAY!
And, Gordie, take your phone just in case.
Okay.
And use the bathroom before you go.
Mom!
Good thinking.

Gordon and Benny hopped on their Big Wheel. They rode up and down the streets. Every chicken they passed wore an itchy sweater and a sad face. Feathers and cookie crumbs covered the ground.

UFO's Land Here!
This is bad, Gordon. Look! Granny Goosebumps has cookie carts all over the city!
It's time to go see Uncle Quack.
ITCH
105
ITCH

Uncle Quack!
We need your help!
Can you tell us
what this is?

Gordon handed Uncle Quack a cookie. Uncle Quack looked at it very carefully. He turned it over. He gave it a sniff.

I've got it!
It's a cookie!

Then Uncle Quack popped the cookie in his mouth.

No!

POOF!
Uncle, you just ate our only clue!
Oh, sorry! I wondered why the cookie was glowing. . . . Is it cold in here?

Gordon told Uncle Quack all about Granny Goosebumps and what had happened at the Fowl Fall Festival.

Now we have to find Granny Goosebumps and stop her before everyone loses their feathers!
Yes, seeing Uncle Quack naked was bad enough.

And we have to help the already naked chickens of the city!
Uncle, can you find a way to regrow feathers?
Yes! It'll be as easy as flying.
But chickens can't fly.

Gordon and Benny ran to their Big Wheel.

To The Beakmobile! 5

Hurry! We have to catch this bad guy and get home by dinnertime.
I'm pedaling as fast as I can!

Gordon and Benny zoomed away from the lab. They were headed back to the Fowl Fall Festival to look for clues. They had to find Granny Goosebumps.

FEATHERLYLESS LOVE
LL FESTIVAL
Canceled due to BAD GUYS!

Gordon and Benny parked the Big Wheel under a tree. There wasn't a chicken in sight. So Gordon let his birdy senses lead the way . . .

. . . and he fell flat on his face. Sometimes Gordon's birdy senses were a pain in the beak. When he opened his eyes, he spotted a clue!

Benny picked up the clue. He took a closer look.

Henny's
fine diner
Early Bird Special
Great Granny Grub!
*Discount Club
This card is the perfect clue! It has Granny Goosebumps's address on the back.
She must have dropped it during our battle!

Gordon and Benny ducked behind a bush. . . .

Ow! Why are leotards so tight?

Kung Pow Chicken and Egg Drop jumped out, ready to kick Granny Goosebumps in the tail feathers!

LET'S GET CRACKING!
KPC
ED

Kung Pow Chicken pressed a button on his Beak-Phone.

The Big Wheel turned into the Beak-Mobile. Kung Pow Chicken pedaled it at top speed.

Trick Or Treat? 6

The superheroes drove to the address on the card.

Stand back!
I'll use my
Power Peck!
PECK
PECK

A granny in a pink housecoat and fuzzy slippers opened the door.

Hello? Oh, is it Halloween
already? What cute costumes!
Costumes?
No, we're real
superheroes!
This is
our way in!
TRICK
OR
TREAT!
KP

The granny went to get candies for the trick-or-treaters. While her back was turned, Kung Pow Chicken and Egg Drop ran past her and into the building.

Wait! She might have candy corn!
No time for snacks! Come on!
KPC
E

They tiptoed down empty hallway,

after empty hallway,

after empty hallway.

The emptiness was spooky. Finally, the heroes turned a corner and heard a scary sound.

Kung Pow Chicken gave Egg Drop a boost so he could peek inside.

Ham and eggs! Every granny in the city must be here. And I see Granny Goosebumps, too!
CLICK
CLICK

Kitchen
OUT
IN
CLICK
CLICK
CLICK
CLICK

Egg Drop leaned forward to get a better look. The door fell open. Kung Pow Chicken and Egg Drop both tumbled into the room.

SWOOSH!
Um, trick or treat?
ZOING!

7 All Tied Up

Granny Goosebumps, you're one bad egg!
Thank you, dearie! Yes, soon my cookies will be all over the city. Every chicken will be naked and cold. They'll need to buy my sweaters! Then I'll have lots of money! And I can finally move to Florida!

Kung Pow Chicken and Egg Drop struggled and strained against the yarn. It was no use. They were wrapped up tight.

Wait! You told us Kung Pow Chicken was behind the naked chickens!
And you said the money you made would go to needy penguins!
You grannies were easy to trick! I sprinkled glowy sugar on your cookies! And getting you to knit sweaters for me was even easier! Ha!

You'll never get away with this!
Want to bet your feathers? Now take a bite of this cookie!

Kung Pow Chicken's beak trembled. He shrank away from the glowing cookie. Then the Beak-Phone rang.

RIINNG!

Kung Pow Chicken squiggled under the yarn. He popped his phone through the strands. It was his mother calling.

You boys are late for dinner! You are both in BIG trouble!!
Mom

That did it. Granny Goosebumps had made Kung Pow Chicken late for dinner. He was mad! It was time to show this bad granny who wore the leotard. It was time to be a superhero. He sucked in a super breath and —

BOK!

FEATHER STORM!

KICK!

You'll do your knitting behind bars now, Granny Goosebumps! Fowladelphia doesn't want your itchy sweaters. And we have the city's biggest brain working on how to regrow feathers!
KPC
RRRIINNNG!
Boys? It's Uncle Quack! Get to the lab NOW!
We're on our way!
Mom's going to be so mad.
KPC

8 How The Cookie Crumbles

Uncle Quack had created a glowy milk. He had dunked himself in it and now his feathers were back fuller than ever! But he didn't know how to get the milk to all the other naked chickens.

It's up to you now, boys.
Hmmm.
I have an idea!

Are you naked? Follow us to Professor Quack's pool party!
Lost your feathers? We can fix that!
MILK
It's Kung Pow Chicken!
There's Ed, too!
Yay!
Our new hero!

Granny Goosebumps had been caught, and the naked chickens were about to regrow their feathers. Kung Pow Chicken and Egg Drop could be ordinary chickens again.

Benny, I'm stuck! Help me get this leotard off!
Whose idea was it for superheroes to wear leotards, anyway?

Gordon and Benny joined Uncle Quack's pool party. Soon, all of the naked chickens had been dunked in the pool of glowy milk. They showed off their fine new feathers.

POOF!
POOF!
POOF!
POOF!
Feather Gro™
You can thank Kung Pow Chicken for your new feathers!
POOF!

FOWLADELPHIA
POOL PARTY!
EXIT
QUACK
LABS
Kung Pow Chicken saved the city. I wish we could find a way to say thanks!
I'm sure he knows, sir.
Candy corn might be nice. . . .

Gordon and Benny rode home as fast as Gordon's chicken legs could go. Mrs. Blue met them at the door.

Gordon and Benedict Blue! I should take away your Big Wheel!
But Uncle Quack called and said you had dinner at the lab. And he said you helped those poor naked chickens I saw on the news!
So you're not in trouble. But next time, you had better call me!
We will, Mom.
Hmmph. It's not my fault. I can't even have a phone!

Then she gave them both a kiss and sent them off to bed.

Gordon and Benny sat on Gordon's bed. They talked about everything that had happened that day. Gordon was proud to finally be a real superhero.

Suddenly, Gordon's tail feathers began to wiggle.

My birdy senses are tingling. . . . Bad guys must be up to no good.
Oh, for peep's sake. He's sitting on his phone.
TINGLE!

LET'S GET CRACKING!

Please take to jail - KPC & ED

Cyndi Marko lives in Canada with her family. She wears a lot of itchy sweaters.

When Cyndi was in second grade, her teacher said her printing was too messy and that she had to practice more. But instead of practicing printing after school, Cyndi would slip into her Wonder Woman costume and red rubber boots. Then she would pedal her purple tricycle around the block at top speed, fighting bad guys! Although Cyndi has since given up crime fighting, she still has messy printing. (Sorry, Mrs. Sieffert!)

Kung Pow Chicken is Cyndi's first children's book series.

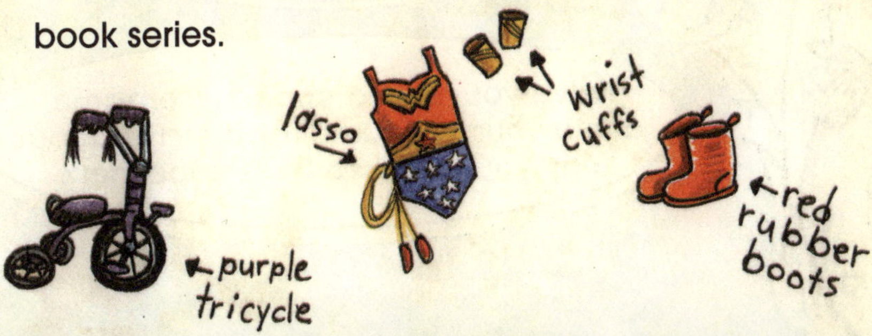

KUNG POW CHICKEN★

Prove your superhero know-how!

How did Gordon and Benny get superpowers?

How does Gordon know when danger is near?

What is Granny Goosebumps's evil plan? And how do Gordon and Benny save the day?

How is Kung Pow Chicken similar to superheroes in other stories?

Give yourself a superhero name, draw your costume, and write about why <u>you</u> want to be a superhero.